W9-BAY-205

ANIMALS AT WORK

Animals
Attacking

WORLD
BOOK

World Book, Inc.
180 North LaSalle Street
Suite 900
Chicago, Illinois 60601
USA

Produced for World Book, Inc. by Bailey Publishing Associates Ltd.

For information about other World Book publications, visit our website at **www.worldbook.com** or call **1-800-WORLDBK (967-5325)**.

Library of Congress Cataloging-in-Publication data has been applied for.

Title: Animals Attacking
ISBN: 978-0-7166-2725-8

Animals at Work
ISBN: 978-0-7166-2724-1 (set, hc)

Also available as:
ISBN: 978-0-7166-2725-8 (e-book)

Printed in China by Shenzhen Wing King Tong Paper Products Co, Ltd., Shenzhen, Guangdong
1st printing August 2018

0078

Staff

Writer: Alex Woolf

Executive Committee

President
Jim O'Rourke

Vice President and Editor in Chief
Paul A. Kobasa

Vice President, Finance
Donald D. Keller

Vice President, Marketing
Jean Lin

Vice President, International
Maksim Rutenberg

Vice President, Technology
Jason Dole

Director, Human Resources
Bev Ecker

Editorial

Director, Print Publishing
Tom Evans

Managing Editor
Jeff De La Rosa

Editor
Will Adams

Manager, Contracts & Compliance
(Rights & Permissions)
Loranne K. Shields

Manager, Indexing Services
David Pofelski

Librarian
S. Thomas Richardson

Digital

Director, Digital Product Development
Erika Meller

Director of Content, Consumer Products
Emily Kline

Digital Product Manager
Jonathan Wills

Manufacturing/Production

Manufacturing Manager
Anne Fritzinger

Proofreader
Nathalie Strassheim

Graphics and Design

Senior Art Director
Tom Evans

Senior Designer
Don Di Sante

Media Editor
Rosalia Bledsoe

Special thanks to:

Roberta Bailey
Nicola Barber
Francis Paola Lea
Claire Munday
Alex Woolf

A lion chases after a zebra. Lions hunt zebra, antelope, and other large mammals throughout sub-Saharan Africa.

Acknowledgments

Cover photo: © Mogens Trolle, Shutterstock

Alamy: title page & 22-23 (Juniors Bildarchiv GmbH), 12-13 (Alessandra Sarti/imageBROKER), 15 (Richardom), 16-17 (Joe Blossom), 18-19 (Reinhard Dirscherl), 19 (Jeff Rotman), 23 (Konrad Wothe/imageBROKER), 24-25 (Sue Clark), 25 (Matthew Banks), 26-27 (Martin Harvey/Gallo Images), 32 (Media Drum World), 33 (Jose B. Ruiz/Nature Picture Library), 37 (Michael & Patricia Fogden/ Minden Pictures), 40-41 (Phil Degginger), 42-43 (Gabbro), 43 (blickwinkel/Teigler), 44 (Manfred Bail/imageBROKER), 45 (Doug Perrine). **Public domain:** 40 (JMK). **Shutterstock:** 5 (Cheryl Ann Quigley), 6-7 (Ian Kennedy), 7 (cellistka), 8 (Pong Wira), 8-9 (Bildagentur Zoonar GmbH), 9 (Alessandro De Maddalena), 11 foreground (Nicolas Primola), 11 background (Klagyivik Viktor), 13 (VisionDive), 14-15 (rokopix), 16 (Tomas Palsovic), 17 (fotoslaz), 20 (Vladimir Wrangel), 20-21 (reptiles4all), 21 (D. Kucharski K. Kucharska), 24 (Tracy Burge), 28 (Aytug askin), 28-29 (wildestanimal), 29 (Tsekhmister), 30-31 (Johanna Veldstra), 31 (Jeannette Katzir Photog), 32-33 (Chris Kruger), 35 (De Paula), 36-37 (Anne Powell), 38 (Dario Sabljak), 38-39 (NaturesMomentsuk), 39 (Sue Robinson), 41 (Martin Pelanek), 42 (Kazakov Maksim), 44-45 (Sista Vongjintanaruks).

Contents

4 Introduction

6 Sensing Prey

12 Weapons

22 Teamwork

26 Chasing

30 Ambushing and Trapping

36 Camouflage and Mimicry

42 Tricks and Treats

46 Glossary

47 Find Out More

48 Index

Introduction

Some animals prey on (hunt) and eat other animals for food. Hunting animals are called **predators,** and they can be found in every part of the world, including polar regions, deserts, rain forests, mountaintops, and oceans. All predators are **carnivores.** In other words, they get their energy from a diet of animal flesh. However, not all carnivores are predators. Some meat-eaters, like vultures and blowflies, are **scavengers**—they feed on flesh of already dead animals. Many predators, such as leopards and wolves, will sometimes scavenge.

Predators play an important role in their **ecosystems.** An ecosystem includes all the living things in a particular environment and the interactions among them. It also includes all the nonliving things that the living things depend on, such as water and **nutrients.** Predators help keep the populations of the **species** they prey on healthy. Lions, for example, often eat old, injured, and sick members of the herds they prey upon. This activity leaves more food for the healthy **prey** and helps to slow the spread of disease within the herd.

In this book, you will learn about the predators of the animal kingdom. You will look at a range of species from a variety of **habitats** and regions of the world. In doing so, you will investigate the tools and tactics they use to seek out, catch, and eat their prey.

FOOD CHAINS

Each predator is part of at least one food chain. A food chain is the process by which energy is passed from one living thing to the next. At the base of a food chain are often plants. They are called producers because they use the sun's energy to produce their own food. Animals are called consumers because they consume plants and other animals, rather than making their own food. Above plants in a food chain are animals called **herbivores,** which eat plants. Next come small predators, such as birds or bugs, that eat the herbivores. Larger predators eat both herbivores and smaller predators. At the top of a food chain are apex predators. No one eats them.

The lion is an example of an apex predator.

Sensing Prey

Before a **predator** can eat another animal, it must find it. Predators use different senses to seek out their **prey.** Many of these, such as eyesight, hearing, smell, and touch, are common throughout the animal kingdom. Others, such as echolocation (see pages 10–11), are used by only a few **species.**

EYESIGHT

Like many predators, eagles have their eyes positioned at the front of their heads. Each eye sees an overlapping and slightly different view of the same scene. This arrangement is called binocular vision, and it gives the eagle good depth perception. In other words, it helps the eagle to determine how far away things are, including prey.

House cats move about at dawn and dusk, and their eyes are well adapted for low-light conditions. A cat's retina, the light-sensing part of the eye, contains a high number of **rod cells,** which are sensitive to light and movement. Cats' eyes also have a tapetum, a layer of **tissue** that reflects light back to the retina, helping to gather more light. This reflection can make a cat's eyes seem to glow at night.

HEARING

Owls have highly developed hearing. They can hear the tiniest movements of their prey in trees, bushes, or snow. Certain species, such as the barn owl, have asymmetrical ears, with one set higher than the other. Sound reaches the ear that is closer to the prey slightly earlier than it reaches the other ear, helping the owl pinpoint the prey's location.

Barn owls have a saucer-shaped ruff of feathers around the eyes, called a facial disk. This structure guides sounds toward the ears.

"Hearing" vibrations

Snakes do not have external (outside the body) ears and eardrums, which allow other animals to hear. Instead, they have inner ears connected to their jawbone. Movements made by prey cause vibrations in the jawbone, which are relayed to the inner ear. The inner ear converts the vibrations into impulses that are then sent to the brain. From this sensory information, the snake is able to work out the distance and direction of the prey.

By resting their jaws on the ground, snakes can pick up vibrations made by prey.

SMELL

The wolf has a powerful sense of smell. It has a long nasal cavity (opening) in its muzzle, above its mouth. This cavity has about 25 times as many smell receptors as the nose of a human being. As a result, wolves can smell their **prey** from a distance of more than a mile (1.6 kilometers).

Badgers are nighttime hunters with poor eyesight, so they rely on their strong sense of smell to locate food. They prey on earth-dwelling creatures, such as ground squirrels, groundhogs, mice, rabbits, and snakes. A badger can sniff out such animals in their burrows through soil and even snow cover.

TOUCH

Spiders are highly sensitive to vibrations, and they use this ability to find prey. Their legs are covered in fine hairs, some of which can feel vibrations in the ground, the air, or even in water.

The fishing spider rests its front legs on the surface of a pond. The hairs on its legs can sense the vibrations made by a struggling **insect** elsewhere in the pond. Orb weaver spiders attach a "signal line" to the center of their webs. When an insect gets caught in the web, the spider feels the signal line vibrate.

Some species of trapdoor spider lay silken "trip lines" around their burrow. When an insect disturbs one of the trip lines, the spider feels the vibration and runs out to capture it.

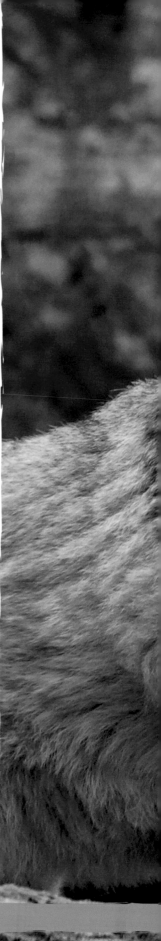

Gray wolves must usually be downwind of a prey animal to catch its scent.

Sensing electric fields

All creatures produce an **electric field** when their muscles contract. Sharks can detect the tiny electric fields produced by prey—for example, by the muscular contraction of a fish's gills. The shark is able to do this using highly sensitive **organs** in its head called ampullae (*am PUHL ee*) of Lorenzini. The ampullae are jelly-filled tubes that open to the water through pores in the shark's skin.

The ampullae of Lorenzini are visible as dark specks on the snout of this blue shark.

Bats and Echolocation

Bats are usually only active at night. To sense their surroundings and hunt for **insects** in the dark, many bats use echolocation. Echolocation is a method that enables bats to sense their surroundings by listening to the returning echoes of their calls. In other words, it allows them to "see" with sound.

A bat can tell the distance to an object by the time it takes for the sound of the bat's call to bounce off the object and return as an echo. By emitting a series of calls, bats can tell objects that must be avoided, such as trees, apart from the insect **prey** that it wants to catch.

Sound waves have a trait called frequency that is related to a sound's pitch. The higher the frequency, the higher the pitch. The calls bats make are mostly at too high a frequency for humans to hear. The highest frequency sound that most humans can hear is around 20 **kilohertz,** whereas bat calls range in frequency from 20 to 200 kilohertz. Low-frequency sounds travel farther than high-frequency sounds. However, bats use high-frequency sounds more often because they give more detailed information about such things as the size of the prey and the speed and direction of its flight.

HORSESHOE BATS focus echolocation calls through horseshoe-shaped structures on their noses.

The volume of sound may be measured in units called decibels. Bat calls can be as loud as 120 decibels, which is louder than a smoke alarm going off 4 inches (10 centimeters) from your ear. We cannot hear such sounds because of their high frequency, but bats can. To avoid being deafened by their own calls, bats contract a muscle in the ear called the stapedius (*stah PEE dee us*) to block much of the sound. The muscle then relaxes a few milliseconds later to enable the bat to hear the echo.

Weapons

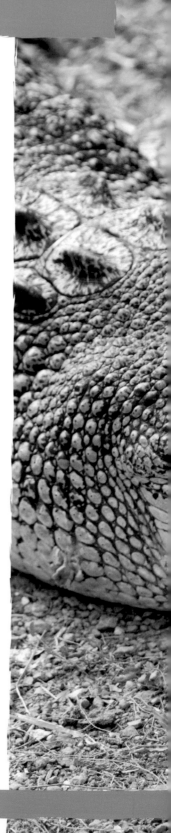

Once a **predator** has found its **prey,** it must catch and eat it. Predators have developed different weapons for catching, stopping, killing, and eating their prey. These weapons include teeth and jaws, beaks, claws, talons, pincers, tentacles, tongues, and **venom.**

TEETH

Many predators, especially **mammals** and **reptiles,** have teeth. Most mammals have at least two types of teeth. These may include incisors, sharp-edged teeth for cutting food, and flat molars, for chewing and grinding. Predatory mammals have long, pointed teeth called canines at the corners of the mouth. Canines are used for grasping prey and for ripping and tearing chunks of flesh. Predators may also use their canines to kill prey with a piercing bite to the throat.

Many fish and most reptiles have just one type of tooth. Sharks, for example, have sharp, slicing teeth, used for biting off pieces of flesh. Snakes swallow their prey whole, so they do not need strong biting teeth. Their teeth curve backward, enabling them to drag their prey toward the throat. Unlike mammals, fish and reptiles regularly shed and regrow their teeth.

JAWS

Predators tend to have jaws with powerful muscles, giving them a strong bite force. Animals with very strong bites include crocodiles, bears, gorillas, hippos, hyenas, jaguars, and sharks. Snakes are not powerful biters, but their jaws have a different feature: the upper and lower jaws are linked by a stretchy band of **tissue,** so they can open very wide. This ability enables a snake to swallow large prey whole.

Suction feeding

Many fish have powerful muscles in their skulls that allow them to open their jaws extremely quickly, greatly expanding the space inside their mouths. This rapid expansion sucks the prey into the fish's mouth.

The frogfish has the fastest known jaw movement of any fish. It can suck in its prey in just six thousandths of a second.

A full-grown saltwater crocodile can bite with a force of 3,700 pounds per square inch (260 kilograms per square centimeter), stronger than any other land animal.

BEAKS

In place of teeth and jaws, birds have a beak. Beaks are lighter than a mouthful of teeth and also streamlined, one of many adaptations that help birds to fly. Beaks vary in shape and size depending on the bird's hunting methods and type of **prey.**

WATER BIRDS

Wading birds often have long, thin beaks. They use them to search for **insects** and **crustaceans** in the mud or sand. The beaks of some fish-eating water birds have serrated (jagged) edges to hold onto slippery, wriggling prey. The black skimmer, a type of shorebird, has a lower beak that extends farther than its upper beak. It hunts by flying low over rivers and lagoons and dipping its lower beak into the water, skimming for fish.

RAPTORS

Raptors, also known as birds of prey, have powerful hooked beaks for grabbing prey. The beaks have sharp edges for cutting and tearing flesh. Most falcons and some kites have a sharp projection along the edge of the upper beak with a matching notch in the lower beak. The projection acts as a "tooth" to cut up their prey.

OTHER ANIMALS WITH BEAKS

Other **species** of **predators** also have beaks. These include some fish, octopuses, squid, and cuttlefish. Many of these creatures eat shellfish as part of their diet, and they use their beaks to break open the shells. Sea turtles also have beaks, which they use to eat many foods. The hawksbill sea turtle's narrow, pointed beak is ideal for pulling prey, such as sponges, out of crevices in a coral reef, whereas the snapping turtle's broad, razor-sharp beak is well-suited for catching fish.

Pufferfish

The pufferfish has powerful, curved teeth—two in its upper jaw and two in its lower jaw—that together form a hard beak. The beak is made up of layers of dentine, a substance also found in human teeth. New layers are continually being formed throughout the pufferfish's life to replace those damaged by eating.

Pufferfish use their beaks to break open clams, mussels, and other shellfish.

As with all raptors, the bald eagle has a hooked upper beak ending in a sharp tip.

CLAWS

Many **predators** of land and air have claws. Predatory **mammals,** such as tigers, use their curved, pointed claws to grasp and hold on to **prey** while they bite them. Birds of prey have powerful hooked claws called talons, which they use in a similar way. Many **reptile** predators— including crocodiles and lizards—also have claws. The only **amphibian species** with claws is the African clawed frog. Moles, hedgehogs, and bears use their claws to dig up **insects.** Big bears, such as the grizzly, sometimes hunt large prey. In such cases, the claw is just the tip of the weapon: one swipe from their powerful paw can break the neck or back of their victims.

Bear claws are long and thin for digging up earth and gripping trees while climbing.

Most species of cat have retractable claws—that is, claws that can be withdrawn into the paw. They may withdraw the claws when walking or running, protecting them from wear and tear. Many cats and dogs also have a "dewclaw" high up on the back of the front paws. Cats can use this claw for grasping prey. Because it does not touch the ground, the dewclaw may be sharper and longer than other claws.

Tigers grab their prey with their claws before delivering a killer bite to the throat.

Pincers

Arthropods are a group of animals that includes insects, **arachnids,** and **crustaceans.** Instead of claws, many species of arthropod have pincers. Pincers are in two parts, somewhat like a pair of jaws. As well as being used for feeding, carrying, and defense, pincers are also often used to attack prey. Crabs, lobsters, and scorpions have pincers at the ends of their front limbs. In the case of insects, pincers are usually part of the **mandible,** an **appendage** near the mouth.

Scorpion pincers are covered in tiny, sensitive hairs. The moment an insect touches one of these, the pincers snap closed, crushing it.

TENTACLES

Some **invertebrates** use tentacles to grab their **prey.** Tentacles are long, flexible limbs containing muscles but no bones. Some **species** of comb jelly have tentacles covered in cells called colloblasts. When a prey animal touches one of these, the colloblasts burst open, releasing sticky threads that trap the creature. The lion's mane jellyfish has the longest tentacles of any animal—the largest recorded specimen had tentacles that reached 120 feet (37 meters) in length. **Venom** in these tentacles stings and **paralyzes** prey. The tentacles then drag the prey to the jellyfish's mouth to be eaten.

The tentacles of the giant squid are lined with hundreds of circular suction cups used to cling to the squid's prey. Each cup has a hard, serrated edge that digs deep into its prey's flesh. The tentacles of the colossal squid also have these powerful suction cups. In addition, the tentacles have rotating hooks at their ends, used for grabbing and holding prey.

RADULAE

Mollusks are a family of invertebrates that includes slugs, snails, squids, and octopuses. In place of a tongue, they have a radula (*RAJ u luh;* plural, *RAJ u lee*)—a flexible **appendage** lined with tiny teeth. They use the radula to shred their food before consuming it, but in some cases it can also be used as a weapon.

The ghost slug uses the long teeth on its radula to grab and eat earthworms. The moon snail, a **predatory** ocean snail, uses the radula together with an acidic secretion to bore through the shells of other mollusks. The cone snail, another type of ocean snail, can launch a **venomous** tooth from its radula as if it was a harpoon. The venom paralyzes its prey, which is then reeled in and eaten.

Squid, which are mollusks, have two long tentacles in addition to their eight arms.

The geographic cone

The geographic cone is the most venomous of all known cone snails. When a small fish, worm, or mollusk approaches, the snail extends a long flexible tube called a proboscis (*proh BOS ihs*). Inside the proboscis is a hollow tooth filled with venom, which the snail fires into its prey with a powerful muscular contraction. The geographic cone swallows the tooth along with its prey. It is constantly growing new teeth, so it is always ready to spear another meal.

This geographic cone has extended its proboscis, ready to fire its poisonous tooth.

VENOM

Venom is a poisonous substance used by some **predators** to stun or kill their **prey.** Snakes and spiders inject venom into their victims by biting them with their fangs. Scorpions, stinging **insects,** and stingrays use stingers. Jellyfish use their tentacles.

Different venoms have different effects on prey. Some venoms may slow or stop the heart, cause internal bleeding, or stop the victim from breathing. Other venoms disable the nervous system, causing numbness or **paralysis,** so the victim can be eaten at the predator's leisure. Spider venom may contain strong digestive juices that can turn an insect's insides to liquid. The spider then uses strawlike mouthparts to suck up the insides.

ELECTRIC SHOCKS

Some fish can give off electric shocks to stun or kill their prey. Such fish include electric eels, electric catfishes, and electric rays. The fish produce these shocks from "electric **organs**" made up of thousands of modified muscle cells called electroplaques (*ee LEK troh placks*). Each of these disc-shaped cells stores a small charge of less than 0.1 volt, but when discharged together they can produce a powerful electric shock.

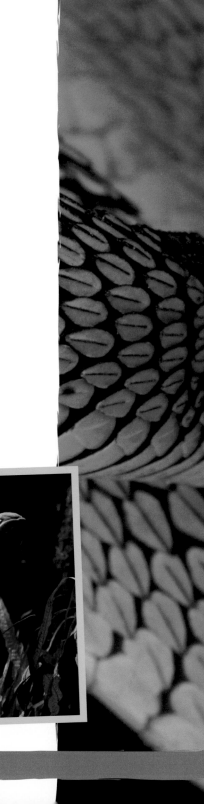

The electric eel of South America can deliver a shock of up to 650 volts, enough to kill a fish or stun a human being.

Spider wasps

The spider wasp uses its sting to **paralyze** a spider. It then drags the spider to a burrow and lays an egg on its body. When the egg hatches, the **larva** eats the spider alive.

A black-banded spider wasp drags its victim, a wolf spider, to its burrow.

Snakes carry their venom in a gland behind the eye. When the snake is ready to bite, the venom passes through a groove or tube to the fang.

Teamwork

Some animals work together to catch their **prey.** Pack hunters include chimpanzees, coyotes, lions, spotted hyenas, and wolves. There are advantages to this approach. Pack hunters can engage in longer hunts because by working as part of a team, each animal uses less energy than it would when hunting alone. Pack hunters can work together to separate weaker or slower individuals from a herd. Working as a pack, **predators** may also take down larger prey than they could alone.

WOLVES

A pack of wolves will often follow a herd of elk or caribou for days before moving in for the kill. They may herd their prey into an area of deep snow, where the heavy, hoofed animals will become bogged down, or onto a dry riverbed, where their prey will stumble on the round pebbles. Lightly built, quicker female wolves may perform the herding role, while the slower, stronger males may carry out the attacks. It may take three or four wolves to bring down a large elk. Hunting in a pack also enables younger wolves to learn hunting skills from older wolves.

SPOTTED HYENAS

Spotted hyenas hunt both alone and in groups, typically of two to five individuals. As a group, they can target bigger prey, such as buffalo and zebras. Working together, they may first separate a mother and calf from the herd. Then, some members of the team will distract the mother while the others attack the small and undefended calf.

Army ants

The army ants of Central and South America live in moving **swarms** numbering 100,000 to 20 million **insects.** The group forms a trail that can be over 330 feet (100 meters) long. Sheer numbers enable them to overwhelm much larger prey, including beetles, scorpions, spiders, snakes, lizards, birds, and small **mammals.**

To cross over a gap, army ants form their bodies into a living bridge.

A pair of spotted hyenas attack an African buffalo.

ORCAS

Orcas, also called killer whales, often travel in groups called pods. Pods work together in different ways to hunt **prey.** When hunting herring, they herd large numbers of fish into a tight, rotating ball near the surface of the water. They slap the ball with their tails, stunning the fish and making them easier to catch.

Like wolves, orcas work in packs to bring down much larger prey, such as gray, humpback, or blue whales. The orcas single out young or weak individuals and take turns ramming and biting the whale and wearing it down. Finally, an orca will launch itself onto the whale's back in an attempt to block its blowhole so it cannot breathe. After a chase that can last hours, the whale eventually drowns.

HARRIS'S HAWK

Unlike most raptors, which hunt alone, the Harris's hawk hunts in groups of two to six birds. Once they have located the prey—which may be a bird, lizard, or small mammal— the hawks fly in an arrowhead formation, with companions to either side of the lead hawk. If the lead hawk dives and misses the prey, one of the companions will take its place, ready to make another attempt.

If the prey takes cover under trees and bushes, several hawks will wade noisily through the brush to flush it out into the open, where others can grab it.

Before a hunt starts, a solitary Harris's hawk will fly ahead and scout for prey.

To attack a seal on an ice floe, orcas will charge at the floe in formation, creating a wave that crashes over the floe and sweeps the seal into the sea.

Yellow saddle goatfish

The yellow saddle goatfish is one of the very few kinds of fish that work together to catch food. While one goatfish chases its prey around a coral formation, others will spread out to block the prey's escape.

Yellow saddle goatfish do not have fixed hunting roles. An individual can be, at different times, a chaser or a blocker.

Chasing

Predators have different ways to catch their **prey.** One of these methods is **stalking** and then chasing prey. Predators that use this method must be capable of great stealth, speed, and agility.

CHEETAH

The cheetah is the fastest of all land **mammals,** with a top speed of 50 to 70 miles (80 to 100 kilometers) per hour. Cheetahs live in the flat, treeless **savanna** of eastern and southern Africa, where speed is a major advantage for a predator. They usually hunt small antelopes such as Thomson's gazelles and impalas.

Cheetahs hide themselves amid the tall grasses of the savanna as they stalk their prey. This behavior enables them to get as close as possible before starting the final sprint. Cheetahs cannot keep up their top speed for long. The chase lasts no more than 60 seconds and often less. Not only are cheetahs quick, they are also agile and can make sudden, sharp turns during the chase as their prey attempts to dodge them.

When a cheetah reaches its prey, it knocks it to the ground with its paw and then kills it with a suffocating bite to the neck. If a cheetah fails to make a kill quickly, it will give up the chase to conserve energy. On average, only 40 to 50 percent of chases end in a kill. After making a kill, the exhausted cheetah must rest beside its victim before it has the strength to drag it to a shaded place and eat it.

BUILT FOR SPEED

The cheetah has light bones and a slender, streamlined body. It has strong legs, padded paws, and semiretractable claws for grip. It has large nostrils and lungs for extra oxygen during a sprint. Its flexible spine works like a spring for its back legs, giving it extra reach during each stride.

The cheetah is capable of sudden bursts of speed, going from 0 to 60 miles (0 to 97 kilometers) per hour in just three seconds.

PEREGRINE FALCON

This falcon can travel faster than any other animal on the planet. It preys on medium-sized birds, such as pigeons, doves, waterfowl, songbirds, and waders. Once it has spotted its **prey,** the peregrine soars to a great height and performs a steep dive, known as a stoop.

During the stoop, the peregrine reaches speeds greater than 200 miles (320 kilometers) per hour. It strikes the prey in mid-air with a clenched foot, stunning or killing it with the impact. If it misses the bird, the peregrine falcon is agile enough to chase it down and catch it in a second attempt. If the prey is too heavy, the falcon will drop it to the ground and eat it there.

The peregrine falcon has traits that help it to withstand the extreme speed and pressure of a stoop. Translucent (see-through) eyelids protect its eyes from debris while allowing it to see. Parts of its beak guide the airflow away from its nostrils to avoid damaging its lungs.

During a stoop, the peregrine folds back its tail and wings and tucks in its feet to make its body more streamlined.

SHORTFIN MAKO SHARK

The fastest shark of all is the shortfin mako. It can reach speeds of at least 30 miles (48 kilometers) per hour in short bursts. Its speed enables it to chase down extremely fast prey, including tuna, swordfish, sailfish, and other sharks. Once it has caught up with its prey, the shortfin mako dives beneath the prey and rushes up at it from below, ripping chunks off its sides and fins.

Dragonfly

The dragonfly is a fast, acrobatic flier. It reaches speeds of 30 miles (48 kilometers) per hour and can make quick, sudden turns in the air. As it flies, the dragonfly holds its legs together to form a basket in which it captures its prey. Instead of directly chasing the prey, the dragonfly will make for a position just in front of the **insect** to catch it.

Dragonflies prey on flying insects, such as midges, mosquitoes, butterflies, and moths.

The shortfin mako's streamlined shape and low-friction scales make it one of the fastest predators in the sea.

Ambushing and Trapping

Some **predators** hunt by staying motionless, often hidden, waiting for the **prey** to come close before the predator pounces. Other predators build traps for their prey. These forms of hunting help the predator to save its energy. But they can be time consuming, as the chances of prey coming within reach may be small. They suit animals with low energy needs that can survive on infrequent meals.

CROCODILE

Crocodiles hunt land animals by sinking their bodies almost completely in the water. They wait like this until an animal comes to the water to drink, then they swim quietly toward it. As soon as the prey is within striking distance, the crocodile surges out of the water, clamps its jaws around the creature's leg or nose, and drags it underwater to drown it.

FISH

Many fish are ambush predators. For example, the alligator gar will lurk near the surface of freshwater lakes and large rivers and wait for a waterfowl, small **mammal,** or turtle to swim by. Then it will sweep upward and grab the prey in its sharp-toothed jaws. The devil scorpionfish lies partially buried in sand on the sea floor. When smaller fish venture close, it springs up and sucks them into its mouth by opening its jaws extremely quickly (see "Suction feeding" on page 13).

Mountain lion

With its powerful back legs, the mountain lion can leap enormous lengths, and it uses this ability to ambush its prey. The mountain lion mainly hunts at night, **stalking** its prey through brush and trees. When it gets close enough, it leaps at the animal, often breaking the prey's neck with a strong bite.

The mountain lion can leap around 40 feet (12 meters).

When crocodiles lie in wait for their prey, often only their eyes and nostrils are visible.

DARTER

The darter, or snakebird, is a bird with a long neck and a sharp beak that eats fish and other aquatic animals. The bird will wait for its **prey** to come close, then dive into the water and impale the creature on its beak. As it attacks, the bird thrusts its neck, head, and beak forward like a throwing spear, giving it extra power in the strike.

ANT LION

Some animals make traps for their prey. An example is the ant lion, an **insect** whose **larva** digs a pit for ants and other small insects to fall into. The ant lion larva first finds a place with dry, sandy soil. Then, using its tail like a shovel, it digs a funnel-shaped hole. When the pit is complete, it buries itself in the sand at the bottom to await its prey. The prey slips on the crumbling, sandy edge of the pit and falls in. The ant lion then comes out and kills it with its jaws.

GLOWWORM

Glowworms are the larvae of several **species** of gnat, native to Australia and New Zealand. They have an **organ** in their **abdomen** that projects a blue-green **bioluminescent** glow, and they use this to attract the insects they prey on. Glowworms live in dark places, such as caves and damp forests. They attach themselves to an overhanging surface, such as a cave roof, and drop strands of silk thread covered in sticky **mucus.** When an insect, lured by the glow, gets trapped on the thread, the glowworm pulls it up and eats it.

Glowworms with their dangling threads light up the roof of this cave in Waitomo, New Zealand.

Bolas spider

The bolas spider hunts by swinging a blob of sticky silk on the end of a line. This weapon, called a bolas, is named after a similar weapon used by ranchers in the South American country of Argentina. The spider hangs onto the edge of a leaf and waits for its prey—a species of moth—to approach. Then it starts to twirl the bolas and traps the moth on the sticky blob.

A female bolas spider with her bolas. The thread is stronger than steel, and few moths escape.

An African darter waits to ambush its prey.

A CLOSER LOOK

Spiders
and their webs

Spiders produce liquid silk from special **glands** in their **abdomen.** They spin the silk into thread using **organs** called spinnerets. The thread can be thin or thick and dry or sticky, depending on the glands and spinnerets the spider uses to make it. Spiders use their silk in different ways. A spider may use its silk as a dragline to lower itself from high places, for example, or as a lining for its burrow.

Many spiders use their silk to build webs to trap their **prey.** Webs come in a number of different forms. Cellar spiders build tangle webs, or cobwebs, a random arrangement of threads found in corners where ceilings meet walls. Tube web spiders build tube-shaped webs. Money spiders build sheet webs, which are flat sheets of silk hung between blades of grass or branches.

The most complex and beautiful of spider webs is the orb web, built by spiders called orb weavers. These are made up of two kinds of silk. One kind is nonsticky, straight threads that run from the web's center to its edges like the spokes of a wheel. The other kind is spiraling lines of sticky threads that connect the spokes. **Insects** get caught in the sticky threads. Spiders avoid getting caught in their own webs by grasping the sticky silk with special hooked claws on their feet.

An **ORB WEAVER** sits in the middle of its web. Web-building spiders can tell the difference between insect prey and other causes of vibration, such as a leaf falling onto the web.

Once the web is built, the spider waits for its prey to land. When an insect lands, the spider senses the impact as a vibration and will make its way toward the trapped prey. Some **species** of orb weaver position themselves in the center of their web. Others find a place to hide nearby, so as to stay hidden from **predators.** They can sense the vibrations caused by the arrival of prey by keeping one foot in contact with a "signal line" attached to the center of the web.

Camouflage and Mimicry

Some **predators** hide themselves from their **prey** using special coloring or shape to blend into the background. This is called **camouflage.** Before the prey animal is aware that the predator is there, it strikes. Another common predator tactic is **mimicry.** In this case, the predator pretends to be something else. It may appear to be something that is not dangerous, such as a tree branch or a rock. In other cases, the predator lures the prey toward it by pretending to be something that the prey animal is attracted to, either to eat or to **mate** with.

LEOPARD

The leopard is an ambush predator, and camouflage is very important to its hunting method. It relies on its prey not seeing it until the prey is close enough for the leopard to pounce. The coloring of the leopard's coat varies depending on its **habitat.** For the leopards of the African **savanna,** a light tan coat offers the best camouflage against dry grasses. Leopards living in the dark, tropical rain forests of Asia have a black coat, helping them to hide in the shadows. The snow leopards native to the mountains of Central and South Asia have smoky grey and white coats to blend in with the snowy landscape.

The spots on a leopard's coat help to break up its outline, making it is less visible against the background.

Gaboon viper

The gaboon viper is a snake that lives in the rain forests and woodlands of **sub-Saharan Africa.** It hunts by spending long periods motionless, waiting for prey to pass by, and then quickly striking with a **venomous** bite. It is pale in color, with tan markings, giving it excellent camouflage against the forest floor.

This gaboon viper is hard to see amid the leaf litter of the rain forest.

ARCTIC FOX

Some birds and **mammals** are able to change their coloring to blend in with their surroundings as the seasons change. One of these is the Arctic fox, which lives in the coastal areas and islands of the Arctic Ocean. During fall and winter, its coat is white to match the snowy landscape. But in spring and summer, its coat is brown or gray, giving it **camouflage** against the earth, rocks, and plants.

OCTOPUS

Some creatures are able to rapidly change the color of their skin to camouflage themselves against a particular background. Octopuses can do this, both to avoid **predators** and to disguise themselves from their **prey.** An octopus's skin contains cells called **chromatophores,** each of which contains a **pigment** of a particular color. By contracting the muscles surrounding the chromatophores, an octopus can change its color.

Some octopuses can even change the texture of their skin to achieve better camouflage when hiding in coral.

BOOMSLANG

The boomslang is a slender, tree-dwelling snake native to the forests of **sub-Saharan Africa.** It feeds on birds, frogs, and lizards, and it has an unusual way of hunting them. When the boomslang sees its prey, it freezes. Then, it starts moving its head slowly from side to side, imitating the branch of a tree swaying in the wind. This trick is an example of **mimicry.** The prey, lulled by this performance, comes closer, and the boomslang attacks with its **venomous** fangs.

The Arctic fox's changing camouflage enables it to sneak up on prey, whatever the time of year.

Crab spider

Crab spiders rely on camouflage and ambush to catch their prey. Some **species** hide within flowers, waiting for **pollinating insects** to visit. Female crab spiders can even change color to match the flower they are on, although it can take several days to make the change.

This bee failed to notice the crab spider lurking within the petals of a flower.

FIREFLY

Some animals use **mimicry** as a way of luring their **prey** toward them. In the case of one **species** of firefly, its prey is lured by the prospect of **mating.** Fireflies are beetles that produce a flashing light to find mates. The males give off a light signal to any nearby females of their species. The females then answer the call with their own light signal. The females of the *Photuris* (*foh TOO rihs*) genus exploit this signaling system to prey on the males of another species. They lure them by imitating the lighting display of the female of that species. When the males arrive, they kill and eat them.

ASSASSIN BUG

Some **predators** use mimicry to lure their prey with the prospect of food. This strategy is used by *Stenolemus bituberus* (*stehn oh LEE mus bih TOOB er us),* a species of assassin bug. This **insect** preys on spiders. It lures them by plucking the strands of their webs with its legs, mimicking the vibrations caused by a trapped insect. Web-building spiders do not have good eyesight—they sense the world mainly through touch as they try to interpret the vibrations of their web. So the assassin bug does not need to worry about being seen as the spider approaches to see what food has landed in its web. When the spider arrives, the assassin bug stabs it with its rostrum (a piercing mouthpart) and eats it.

Stenolemus bituberus, a species of assassin bug, spends its entire life in spider webs.

Northern shrike

The northern shrike is a large songbird of the Northern Hemisphere. Among its prey are smaller songbirds, and it sometimes lures them by mimicking their calls. It hides itself in trees or brush as it makes these calls, waiting for a flock of them to gather. As they flit about in search of the source of the familiar call, the shrike suddenly flies out and grabs one of the birds in its beak.

Once it has caught its prey, the northern shrike often impales it on sharp twigs, thorns, or barbed wire to make it easier to consume.

Each species of firefly has its own unique light signal.

Tricks and Treats

In addition to **camouflage** and **mimicry, predators** use many other kinds of trickery to tempt their **prey** into range. Some play dead, whereas others use distraction. One common form of deception is to offer prey something that looks like a tasty treat.

CICHLID FISH

A **species** of cichlid fish from Lake Malawi in eastern Africa will pretend to be dead to attract prey. The Livingston's cichlid will sink to the bottom of the lake and lie motionless on its side. When smaller fish arrive to feast on what appears to be the remains of a dead fish, the cichlid jerks back to life and attacks the **scavengers.**

The blotchy coloring of the Livingston's cichlid helps give it the appearance of a rotting carcass.

HERON

Some kinds of wading birds called herons use bait to catch their prey. Striated herons, for example, have been observed dropping **insects,** spiders, seeds, berries, and other floating objects on the surface of the water and then catching fish attracted by them. If the bait drifts away, the heron grabs it and places it back where it saw fish surface earlier. It may also scare away other birds attracted by the bait.

Tentacled snake

The tentacled snake, a water-dwelling snake that lives in southeast Asia, has developed a hunting method based on distracting its prey. The snake adopts the shape of a "J" with its head and neck curved away from the rest of its body. When a fish comes within range, the snake flexes its body, creating a disturbance in the water. The fish darts away from the disturbance and straight into the waiting jaws of the snake.

A striated heron, having laid its insect bait, waits for a fish to surface.

The tentacled snake uses the movement of its body to trick its prey toward its mouth.

DEATH ADDER

Many **predators** lure their **prey** by offering up a part of their body that looks like a tasty morsel of food. One such animal is a snake called the death adder. Its tail has a brightly colored tip that looks like a wriggling worm or grub. The adder hunts by covering itself with leaves so that only the twitching, wormlike tip of its tail remains visible. It waits like this, often for several days. When a prey animal approaches to investigate, the death adder strikes.

ALLIGATOR SNAPPING TURTLE

The alligator snapping turtle is a freshwater turtle that lives in the southeastern United States. It is an ambush predator that hunts by sitting motionless on the bottoms of murky rivers with its jaws open. Its tongue has a fleshy **appendage** that looks like a small red worm. The turtle sits like this, displaying its lure and waiting for a curious fish to come close enough to be eaten.

WOBBEGONG SHARK

The wobbegong shark lives in the shallow waters around Australia and and the southeast Asian country of Indonesia. Also known as the carpet shark, it spends most of its life on the sea floor. It lies very still, and the markings on its back help to **camouflage** it, making it look like part of the seabed.

The wobbegong has fleshy appendages around its jaws that attract small fish because they look like seaweed. When the fish come to nibble on the "seaweed," the wobbegong opens its wide, powerful jaws and eats them.

Anglerfish

The anglerfish attracts prey using a spine that sprouts from its snout. It uses this spine much like an angler uses a fishing rod. At the tip of the spine there is a small fleshy growth called an esca, which the anglerfish waves around as a lure. This action draws the curious prey close, where it can be snatched up.

Some deep-sea anglerfish species give off bioluminescent light from their esca.

Prey, such as minnows, are attracted to the wriggling appendage on the alligator snapping turtle's tongue.

Glossary

abdomen the rear part of an arthropod's body.

amphibian a vertebrate with scaleless skin that usually lives part of its life in water and part on land. Vertebrate animals have a backbone.

appendage a projecting part of an animal.

arachnid a group of arthropods that includes spiders and scorpions.

arthropod a very large group of invertebrates that includes insects, arachnids, and crustaceans.

bioluminescent describing a light emitted by such living things as glowworms and deep-sea fish. It is caused by a chemical reaction involving a light-emitting pigment within the creature.

camouflage the natural coloring or form of an animal that enables it to blend into its surroundings, making it difficult to see.

carnivore a meat-eating animal.

chromatophore a cell in an animal's skin that contains pigments, enabling the animal to alter its coloring.

crustacean a group of mainly aquatic arthropods that includes crabs, lobsters, shrimps, and barnacles.

ecosystem a system made up of a group of living things and its physical environment, and the relationship between them.

electric field an area around an electrically charged object. Any charged particle or object entering that area will feel a force, as will the original object.

gland an organ in an animal's body that secretes (gives off) chemical substances for use in the body or for release into the surroundings.

habitat the place where a living thing usually makes its home.

herbivore a plant-eating animal.

insect one of the major invertebrate groups. Insects have six legs and a three-part body.

invertebrate an animal without a backbone.

kilohertz a measure of frequency equivalent to 1,000 cycles per second.

larva (plural larvae) the active, immature stage of some animals, such as many insects, that is different from its adult form.

mammal one of the major vertebrate animal groups. Vertebrate animals have a backbone. Mammals feed their offspring on milk produced by the mother, and most have hair or fur.

mandible either half of the crushing organ in an arthropod's mouthparts.

mate the animal with which another animal partners to reproduce (to make more animals like the two that are mating); the act of mating, when two animals come together to reproduce.

mimicry the action of imitating something, or the close external resemblance of an animal to something else.

mollusk a group of invertebrates that includes slugs, snails, mussels, and octopuses.

mucus a thick liquid that is produced in parts of animals' bodies.

nutrient a substance that is needed to keep a living thing alive and help it to grow.

organ a part of the body, made of similar cells and cell tissue, that performs a particular function.

paralysis the loss of the ability to move.

paralyze to make a living thing unable to move.

pigment the natural coloring matter of animal tissue.

pollinate to put pollen into a flower or plant so that it produces seeds.

predator an animal that hunts, kills, and eats other animals.

prey an animal that is hunted, killed, and eaten by another.

reptile one of the major vertebrate animal groups. Vertebrate animals have a backbone. A reptile has dry, scaly skin and breathes air. Snakes, crocodiles, and lizards are all reptiles.

rod cells one of two kinds of light-sensitive cell in the retina of an animal's eye. Rod cells are responsible mainly for monochrome (black, white, and gray) vision in poor light. (The other type is the cone cell, responsible mainly for color vision in bright light.)

savanna grasslands with widely scattered bushes and trees.

scavenger an animal that feeds on the carcasses of dead animals.

species a group of living things that have certain permanent traits in common and are able to reproduce with each other.

stalk to pursue in a stealthy manner.

sub-Saharan Africa the part of Africa south of the Sahara Desert.

swarm a large group of arthropods moving together either in search of food or a new home.

tissue the material of which living things are made.

venom a naturally produced liquid that animals can introduce into other animals (for example, through biting) in order to stun, injure, or kill the other animal.

venomous describes an animal that produces venom or a part of such an animal that releases venom.

BOOKS

Deadly Predators by Melissa Stewart (Collins, 2017)

Electric Eel (Apex Predators of the Amazon Rainforest) by Ellen Lawrence (Bearport Publishing, 2017)

Trap-Door Spiders and Other Amazing Predators by Rebecca E. Hirsch (Lerner, 2017)

Sharks: Predators of the Sea by Anna Claybourne (Firefly, 2016)

WEBSITES

American Museum of Natural History – Crocs
http://www.amnh.org/exhibitions/crocs
Take an in-depth look at the evolution, biology, and behavior of crocodiles.

Australian Museum – Predators, Parasites and Parasitoids
https://australianmuseum.net.au/predators
-parasites-and-parasitoids
Learn about predators and other kinds of species that use other animals as food, how they hunt, and why they are important for the environment.

BBC Nature Wildlife – Predator
http://www.bbc.co.uk/nature/adaptations/Predation
Find information and watch videos about a wide range of predators.

Easy Science for Kids – Small Predators
http://easyscienceforkids.com/animals/mammals
/small-predators/
Discover a little about some of the smaller predatory mammals.

African clawed frogs   16
alligator gars   30
anglerfish   45
ant lions   32
arctic foxes   38, 39
army ants   23
arthropods   17

badgers   8
bats   10–11
  horseshoe bats   11
beaks   12, 14, 15, 28, 32, 41
bears   12, 16
birds   6, 7, 14, 15, 16, 23, 24, 28,
  32, 33, 41, 42 ,43
biting   12, 13, 16, 17, 20, 21, 24,
  26, 31, 37
black skimmers   14

cats   6, 16
cheetahs   26–27
claws   12, 16, 17, 26, 34
coyotes   22
crocodiles   12, 13, 16, 30, 31
  saltwater crocodiles   13

darters   32, 33
devil scorpionfish   30
dragonflies   29

eagles   6, 15
  bald eagles   15
echolocation   6, 10–11
ecosystems   4
electric eels   20
electric field, sensing of   9
electric shocks   20
eyesight   6, 8, 28, 40

fireflies   40, 41

fish   12, 13, 14, 15, 20, 25, 30,
  31, 42, 45
food chains   4
frogfish   13

ghost slug   18
glowworms   32

Harris's hawk   24
hearing   6, 7, 11

insects   17, 20, 23, 29, 32, 40, 41

jaws   7, 12, 30, 32, 44
jellyfish   18, 20
  comb jellies   18
  lion's mane jellyfish   18

killer whales   24, 25

leopards   4, 36, 37
lions   4, 5, 22
Livingston's cichlid fish   42

mountain lions   31

northern shrikes   41

octopuses   14, 18, 38
owls   6, 7
  barn owls   6, 7

peregrine falcons   28
pincers   17
pufferfish   15

radulae   18

scorpions   17, 20, 23
sharks   9, 12, 28, 29
  blue sharks   9
  shortfin makos   28, 29
  wobbegong sharks   44
smell, sense of   8, 9

snails   18, 19
  cone snails   18, 19
  moon snails   18
snakes   7, 12, 20, 21, 37, 38, 43, 4
  boomslangs   38
  death adders   44
  gaboon vipers   37
  tentacled snakes   43
spider wasps   21
spider webs   34–35, 40
spiders   8, 20, 23, 34–35
  bolas spiders   33
  crab spiders   39
  fishing spiders   8
  orb weavers   8, 34, 35
  trapdoor spiders   8
spotted hyenas   22, 23
squid   14, 18, 19
  colossal squid   18
  giant squid   18
Stenolemus bituberus   40
stingrays   20
stings   20, 21
striated herons   42, 43
suction feeding   13, 30

teeth   12, 14, 15, 18, 20, 30
tentacles   18, 20
tigers   16, 17
turtles   14, 44, 45
  alligator snapping turtles   44,
    45
  hawksbill turtles   14
  snapping turtles   14

venom   18, 19, 20, 21, 38

wolves   4, 8, 9, 22
  gray wolves   9

yellow saddle goatfish   25